# ACTION MAN

## EXTREME SPORTS

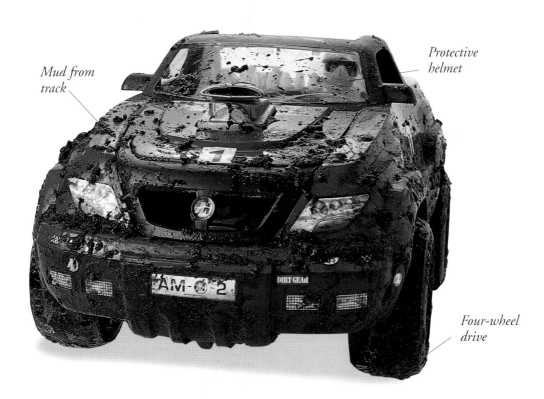

Mud from track

Protective helmet

Four-wheel drive

A DORLING KINDERSLEY BOOK

# CONTENTS

## HOW THIS BOOK WORKS

*There are three types of spread:*
- **Sports** *is about extreme sports*
- **Training** *covers extreme locations (and tells you about the characters)*
- **Missions** *take you right into Action Man's world of extreme sports*

**TRAINING**

*Use the **datafiles** to find other pages to turn to.*

**SPORTS**

*The **top bar** displays the type of spread (X Sports, Training, or Mission).*

*Buttons pop up when a fact box is displayed.*

*Look out for **fact boxes** about places, nature, sport, skills, etc.*

*Mission files show at-a-glance facts about each mission.*

**MISSION**

# LET'S GO!

Action Man is the world's greatest action hero. He competes in the most extreme sports the world has ever seen. He trains hard and plays to win. However, just as important to Action Man is the sheer thrill of taking part: the mind-blowing speed, the heart-stopping risks, the cool tricks.

Even after the race, the adventure doesn't stop. Because wherever Action Man goes, a sinister figure follows, creating all kinds of havoc. This menacing villain is Dr. X, and only Action Man can stop him...

JOIN THE RIDE!

Action Man is a sports superstar with a fast-paced lifestyle. He takes part in the Acceleration Games, a series of next-level extreme events. When he's not competing, he trains, tries new sports, and hangs out with his crew.

Action Man has never revealed how he got his scar.

**STAYING IN SHAPE**
Action Man stays in shape by doing sit-ups and pushups. He needs to be in good shape because extreme sports are very physically demanding.

Action Man's body reflexes are faster than average.

On his left arm, Action Man has a tattoo of his logo.

**COOL GEAR**
Action Man is a gadget fanatic. Much of his sports gear is specially modified to go faster and "up the thrill-factor."

Snowboard

## SKILLS

• Action Man has a unique (and mysterious) ability to respond to extreme danger and stress with lightning-fast reflexes.

• When faced with a seemingly impossible situation, Action Man thinks through all the options in an instant and chooses the best one.

The Daily News

**ACTION MAN RACES TO GLORY!**

Action Man's speed and inventiveness make headlines in newspapers and on the internet. He even has his own site at www.actionman.com!

**INFOSEARCH**
- FIND OUT MORE ABOUT THE SINISTER DR. X ON PAGES 8-9.
- DISCOVER LOTS MORE ABOUT EXTREME SPORTS AROUND THE WORLD ON THE NEXT PAGE.

*Link to the internet*

*Radar dish*

*Laptop computer*

**DATA**

- Action Man's support crew is the Team Xtreme, who back him up in the Acceleration Games.

- Grinder is Team Xtreme's pilot, mechanic, and amateur philosopher. Fidgit is the team's official photographer, always looking for the "killer shot." Rikki is the manager and all-around businessman.

Action Man's support crew uses high-tech communications equipment to keep in contact with each other during extreme competitions.

*Headphones*

*Wide side mirror*

*Customized biker helmet with horns*

OLD RIVALS Dr. X is an evil criminal mastermind. While he tries to cause mayhem, Action Man uses his intelligence, special gear, and sports skills to overcome him.

*Malicious kick*

*Chopper-style fork*

# WORLDWIDE SPORTS

ARCTIC MISSION
PAGES 46-47

## SNOWBOARDING

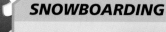

Mount Snow in Vermont has played host to the Winter Extreme Games. More than 83,000 spectators watch snowboarding (see pages 42-43) and other extreme winter sports.

## SKATEBOARDING

The Summer 2000 Extreme Games were held in San Francisco. One of the most popular events was skateboarding (see page 12).

**NORTH AMERICA**

Rocky Mountains

Chihuahuan Desert

Appalachian Mountains

Central American Rain forest

**ATLANTIC OCEAN**

SKYDIVE MISSION
PAGES 20-21

JUNGLE MISSION
PAGES 20-21

Amazon Rain forest

**SOUTH AMERICA**

Andes Mountains

Shoe clip

$E$xtreme sports are a faster, riskier alternative to traditional sports. People who play them travel the world in search of the most extreme landscapes they can find. Extreme sports events are held worldwide, too. The most famous is the X (Extreme) Games.

## KAYAKING

South America has many opportunities for extreme kayaking (see pages 38-39), including the world's second longest river—the Amazon in Brazil.

**SPORTS**

# SPORTS

## SKYDIVING

Speed skydiving (see pages 20-21) is the fastest non-motorized sport on Earth! The 2000 world champion came from France.

## CLIMBING

The 10 highest mountains in the world lie in the Himalayas in Asia. The tallest is Mount Everest. Talk about extreme climbing! (See pages 32-33.)

### EXTREME SPORTS

- Extreme sports are different from traditional sports. The athletes competing in them are not judged by how far they can throw a ball or how fast they run around a track.

- Winning is not the most important factor for extreme sports athletes. They also prize creativity and determination.

- Remember, extreme athletes are trained professionals—don't try to copy any of the moves you see in this book at home!

EUROPE

ASIA

Carpathian Mountains

SKATEBOARD MISSION
PAGES 14-15

Gobi Desert

PACIFIC

OCEAN

Caucasus Mountains

Himalayas

Atlas Mountains

DESERT MISSION
PAGES 36-37

Southeast Asian Rainforest

## KUNG FU

Sahara Desert

Arabian Desert

Kung Fu (see pages 26-27) began in China long ago. Experts can perform great feats of strength by focusing their minds.

AFRICA

African Rain forest

INDIAN

OCEAN

Great Rift Valley

OCEAN MISSION
PAGES 20-21

AUSTRALIA

Australian Desert

Kalahari and Namib Deserts

## INLINE SKATING

Inline skating (see page 12) is featured in more than 100 extreme events around the world each year. South Africa hosts a famous extreme downhill event.

## STREET LUGE

In summer 2000, Sydney in Australia held the first world championship for street luge (see page 13). Riders hit speeds of more than 70 miles per hour.

KEY TO THE WORLD'S MOST
EXTREME LOCATIONS

☐ DESERT

☐ RAIN FOREST

☐ MOUNTAIN

☐ ICE

MISSION LOCATIONS

Strap supports infrared eyepiece

**D**r. X is the world's most evil criminal mastermind. His plan is to create the "next level" of humans, who will take over the world. He is quite capable of destroying the rest of humanity to achieve this goal.

Arm joined to shoulder with cables

**MAD SCIENCE**
Dr. X was once a brilliant scientist who attempted to create a "super-human," with extraordinary strengths. Now, he'll do anything to discover the secret of Action Man's amazing athletic skills.

Bolted armor plating

Powerful robotic arm can punch through walls

Super-absorbent suspension

Steel-capped heavy-duty boots

Dr. X uses miniature robots known as trilobugs to deliver messages and spy on people. When their job is done, they self-destruct.

Toxic guts

Release wheel

• When his research project was closed down, Dr. X lost control and blew up the research faculty.

• Dr. X's body was horribly damaged in the blast. He is now a living cyborg—a terrifying mix of human and machine parts.

• He relies on Professor Gangrene to repair and improve his cyborg parts.

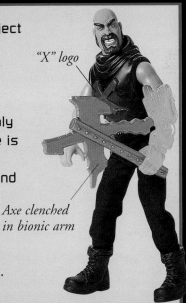

"X" logo

Axe clenched in bionic arm

## HISTORY

Customized helmet (horns added by Dr. X)

Dazzling headlight

Dr. X always seems to be one step ahead of the authorities. He travels between his secret bases using customized vehicles such as submarines and helicopters. He also burns up the streets on a souped-up chopper.

Extra-loud exhaust

Shin deflector on race boot

Fat tires grip the road

Professor Gangrene is Dr. X's chief creator of malicious machines and toxic mayhem. Once a respectable scientist, Gangrene's greed soon got the better of him. Luckily for Dr. X, the foul fanatic is very weak-willed. Otherwise, Dr. X would have a serious rival in crime.

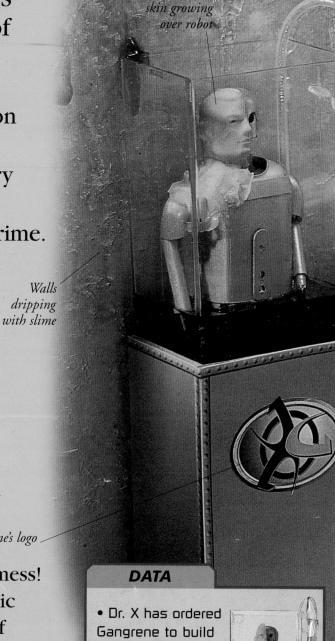

Artificial skin growing over robot

Walls dripping with slime

Gangrene's logo

## MYSTERIOUS ORIGINS

Little is known about the early life of this corrupt chemist. Files indicate that he was experimenting with radioactivity in space when something went wrong. As a result, his skin was turned a nearly luminous green.

TOXIC BLASTER

## THE LABORATORY

Gangrene's lab is like his mind—a frantic mess! High-voltage machines hum and whirr. Toxic slime drips from the walls and parts of unfinished experiments litter every surface. Gangrene is valuable to Dr. X because he is reckless enough to build anything his master requires.

*In the past, Dr. X has also been helped by a street thug known only as Maxx. His head is covered with bandages after one of Gangrene's experiments blew up in his face.*

## DATA

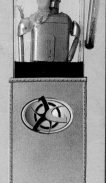

• Dr. X has ordered Gangrene to build a super-robot. He wants it to look and act just like Action Man.

• Gangrene has already created a body frame. Now he is trying to grow an artificial skin over it.

- Status: Second in command to Dr X
- Skills: Robotics and bizarre chemistry
- Unusual body features: toxic guts and bionic eye

*Main computer*

*High voltage dispersal unit*

*Gangrene is building a new robotic arm for Dr. X*

## EQUIPMENT

- Most human body parts can be replaced by artificial ones.

- Robotic hands operate with greater strength and precision than human hands ever could.

*Robotic fingers*

*"CATCH SOME REALLY BIG AIR!"*

Elbow pad

Safety mask

Hand grips board

*"Big air" (all four wheels off the ground)*

Skateboarding and inline skating started as street pastimes. Now they are both organized sports with their own superstars and high-profile competitions. Action Man is world class in both, and has invented many new tricks.

SKATE TRICKS

Skateboarders leap onto and over obstacles, doing flips and turns in the air—all at top speeds. However easy it looks, it takes lots of practice and skill to do even the simplest tricks.

*Action Man's off-road skateboard is a radical design. Its large wheels can handle grass and rough surfaces. It is also motorized to give him an extra edge in races.*

Engine

Bindings support feet

Board    Rear suspension

## SKILLS

• The basis for most skateboard stunts is a jump called an ollie. It allows skateboarders to skim over obstacles and onto curbs.

• Action Man is doing a trick called a grind. The board slides along a railing or the edge of a step or curb.

*Skateboard doing a grind*

*Railing*

## INLINE SKATING

Extreme inline skating is exciting to watch and exhilarating to do. Skaters jump off launch ramps, ride stairs, and grind rails. Action Man is throwing a trick called a Sad Plant Invert. He is hanging onto the top of a curved ramp known as a quarter pipe.

INFOSEARCH
- MANY SKATEBOARDERS ALSO LOVE TO SNOWBOARD. SEE PAGES 10-11.
- SEE ACTION MAN'S MOTORIZED INLINE SKATES ON PAGE 25.

*All-important knee pads*

*Action Man throws a trick called a Sad Plant Invert*

*"LIVE ON THE EDGE!"*

*In street luge, athletes lie flat on a board just a few inches above the ground. They hurtle down hills at speeds of more than 70mph – as fast as a car traveling on a highway. Luge boards, however, have no brakes!*

*Riders travel downhill feet first*

*Inline skates also used for street luge*

STREET LUGE

*Skate shorts*

RAPPEL

*Action Man's inline skates can also be used to rappel down a building or mountain.*

### SPORTS

• Some inline skating tricks are similar to those in skateboarding. Skaters need to build up great speed to propel themselves into the air to do stunts.

• Young inline skaters often compete on an amateur circuit. This is the start of the route to becoming a professional skater.

*Action Man controls his skateboard in the air*

*Gangrene takes aim, unaware of who is behind him*

**BZZZT!**

*Toxic fuel cell full of green gunk*

*Deadly germ spray*

**A**ction Man arrived in Paris. It was the day of an extreme skateboard race across the city's rooftops and Action Man was taking part. As he got ready, Action Man looked around for signs of Dr. X. Suddenly, a flash of light caught his eye. Squinting upward, Action Man saw the vile shape of Gangrene aiming a germ spray at the crowd!

## Rooftop race

Wasting no time, Action Man skated over the roofs and crash-landed on top of Gangrene. "It's not me you want," Gangrene hissed. "I'm just creating a diversion. You won't catch Dr. X now. He's stealing parts for a super satellite." But where was Dr. X?

*"I'm taking this toxic fuel cell off you.*

*Do you recognize the face at the window?*

*Action Man used an air duct as a ramp*

MISSION DR. X – SUPER THIEF
LOCATION PARIS, FRANCE

**RACE CIRCUIT**

**PARIS**
SKATEBOARDERS LOVE PARIS, THE
CAPITAL OF FRANCE. IT HAS SOME
EXCELLENT SKATEBOARD PARKS.

**MISSION STATS**

EXTREME SKATEBOARD
SPEED: 62 MPH
WEAPONS: 2 DISCS

GRINDER
SUPPORT
BACK UP

PROCEED

## Take to the skies

Action Man thought quickly.
Where would Dr. X steal electronic
parts? Then he remembered the
factory on the edge of the city.
Action Man called his backup team.
"I need a gyrocopter—and fast!"
Minutes later he was flying
toward the factory.
His onboard satellite
sensors started buzzing.
"Looks like there's been a break-in."
At that moment, he saw Dr. X
escaping along an alley.

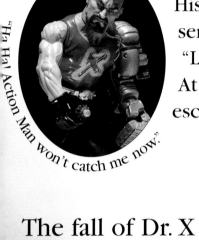

*"Ha Ha! Action Man won't catch me now."*

## The fall of Dr. X

"Time to replace wings for
wheels," said Action Man. He
landed the gyrocopter and
jumped on his skateboard.
When Dr. X was in sight, Action
Man launched a firing disc.
Dr X stumbled and the stolen
detonator went flying. Action Man
snatched it to safety, but Dr. X
escaped. "That's defused his plans,"
said Action Man. "But he'll be back..."

*Disc-firing
motor*

*The stolen electronic
detonator goes flying*

*The ground
shakes as
Dr. X stumbles*

*Spinning
disc trips
up Dr. X*

*Neighboring
rooftops*

CRASH!

# EXTREME BIKING

Two wheels are the way to go! Mountain bikes are built to handle off-road conditions such as deep mud and steep mountainsides. Motorcycles also race in wild locations including ice tracks. Both raise the tension with top speeds and hot stunts.

*"GET OFF THE ROAD!"*

*In cross-country races, riders carry their mountain bikes across rivers and other obstacles. It's all part of the challenge of extreme sports.*

## MOUNTAIN BIKING

Downhill racing is an adrenaline-packed form of mountain biking. All that you need are unshakeable balance, plenty of nerve, and tons of determination!

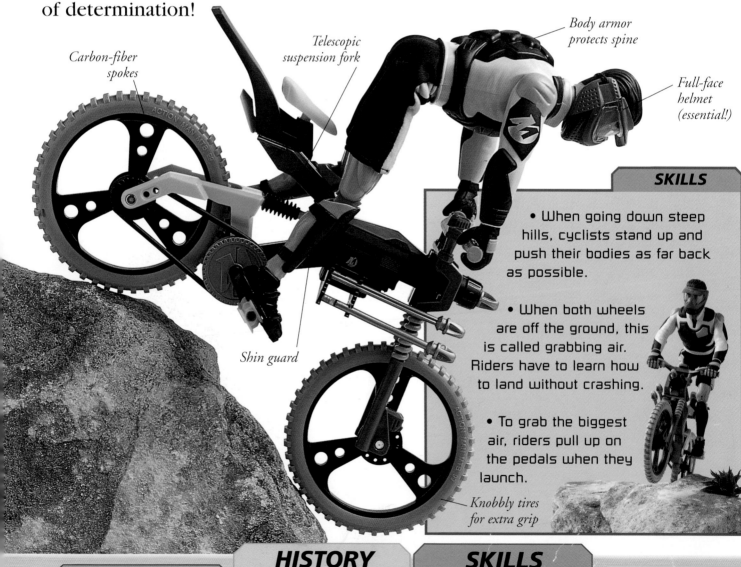

*Carbon-fiber spokes*

*Telescopic suspension fork*

*Body armor protects spine*

*Full-face helmet (essential!)*

*Shin guard*

*Knobbly tires for extra grip*

### SKILLS

• When going down steep hills, cyclists stand up and push their bodies as far back as possible.

• When both wheels are off the ground, this is called grabbing air. Riders have to learn how to land without crashing.

• To grab the biggest air, riders pull up on the pedals when they launch.

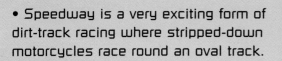
- Speedway is a very exciting form of dirt-track racing where stripped-down motorcycles race round an oval track.

  - The bikes have no brakes, so riders slow down by sliding their machines through turns.

SPORTS

## INFOSEARCH

- WARNING: FOR DANGEROUS DATA ON DR. X'S EVIL MOTORCYCLE, TURN STRAIGHT TO PAGE 9.
- WHERE DOES ACTION MAN RIDE HIS SUPERBIKE? SEE PAGE 26.
- CHECK OUT ALL THE FACTS ON ACTION MAN'S MOTORIZED INLINE SKATES. SEE PAGE 25.

## ICE RACING

Ice racing is a spectacular and dangerous motorcycle sport. Bikes are equipped with spiked tires to grip the slippery ice. Action Man's ultracool ice bike is designed for long-distance, cross-country ice racing.

*Helmet goggles*

*Wheel chains for gripping ice*

*Throttle on right-hand grip controls speed*

*Buildup of ice on the engine*

*Mud guard*

*Chest guard*

## MOTOCROSS

Motocross is also known as "scrambling." Races take place on muddy tracks with lots of slopes and bumps. Action Man's motocross bike has seen plenty of messy action!

*Knobbly tires grip loose ground*

### HISTORY

- BMXs are small stunt bikes that were popular in the 1970s. Now they feature in many extreme sports events.

# AUTO RACING

Auto racing is a fast and dangerous sport. Race cars reach speeds of 250 miles per hour as they race around a curving track. Cars use the latest automotive inventions to reach these fearsome speeds. The drivers are very skilled and brave.

*Fire-resistant mask (worn under helmet)*

*Sponsor logo*

*Hasbro*

*MICRO PROSE*

ACTION MAN

*The most crucial part of a racing driver's clothing is the helmet. It is made from extremely hard-wearing materials to protect the driver's head.*

*Front visor*

## RACE CAR

Race cars are built for speed. They are specially shaped to slice through the air. The body and engine are made from ultralight materials to help them go as fast as possible.

*Cap*

*Heavy-duty racing suit*

*Wide, smooth tires called "slicks"*

*Lightweight body shell*

*Driving shoes*

*Eagle decoration*

INFOSEARCH
READ ABOUT ACTION MAN'S
OTHER FAST CARS:
DESERT JEEP, PAGE 35
SILVER SPEEDER, PAGES 24-25
JUNGLE JEEP, PAGE 29

## EQUIPMENT

• Pit mechanics use a quick jack to raise the car so they can change the wheels.

• Mechanics carry all the right tools to make repairs and fine-tune the car so it performs at its very best.

## PIT-LANES

Pit-lanes are noisy, busy areas at the side of the track for servicing and refueling vehicles. Pit mechanics work as fast as they can to get the car back into the race. Race cars have electrical sensors inside them, which constantly relay information to the pit mechanics about the car's performance.

*Fuel injector*

*Quick jack*

*Pit mechanic refuels the car*

*Aerofoil stops car from flipping over at high speeds*

*Crash barrier*

*Mechanic's toolbox*

The sky is the biggest stadium there is! It is the only place where athletes can move their bodies in every direction, even up and down. Air sports fanatics surf, glide, and soar through the air in defiance of gravity, and at great speed.

*Helmet-mounted camcorder*

## SKYSURFING

Skysurfers leap out of an airplane at 12,800 feet above the ground riding a specially designed skyboard. Before opening their parachute, they slide, spin, twist, and surf through the sky.

*Breathing equipment*

*"SURF THE ULTIMATE WAVE!"*

*Lightweight jumpsuit*

*Glove*

## SKILLS

• Skysurfers jump with a camcorder operator, who must twist around and under the skysurfer to get the best possible shots.

• A single jump lasts just 70 seconds. For the first 50 seconds, the skysurfer is traveling at up to 140 mph.

**SKILLS**

*Skyboard*

*Winch*

*Cockpit with automatic flight control system*

### INFOSEARCH
☐ LEARN MORE ABOUT SKYDIVING ON PAGE 7.
☐ NOW SEE ACTION MAN USE HIS SKYDIVING SKILLS TO SURPRISE DR. X...ON THE NEXT PAGE!

*Action Man is a trained helicopter pilot. Student pilots must complete many hours of training flights. They also learn how to land a helicopter in emergency situations.*

## SPORTS

• Skydiving parachutists "freefall" for thousands of feet. They link hands in formation before opening their parachutes to land safely on the ground.

• Speed skydivers freefall headfirst in order to reach the fastest speeds.

*Rigid wing*

*Steering grip*

*Parachute is opened at the last moment*

## HANG GLIDING

Hang gliders are special aircraft, shaped like a pair of wings. They don't need power to fly, but are carried along by the wind. Action Man's hang glider is an unusual shape. It is steered by hand grips, and reaches heights of more than 18,000 feet.

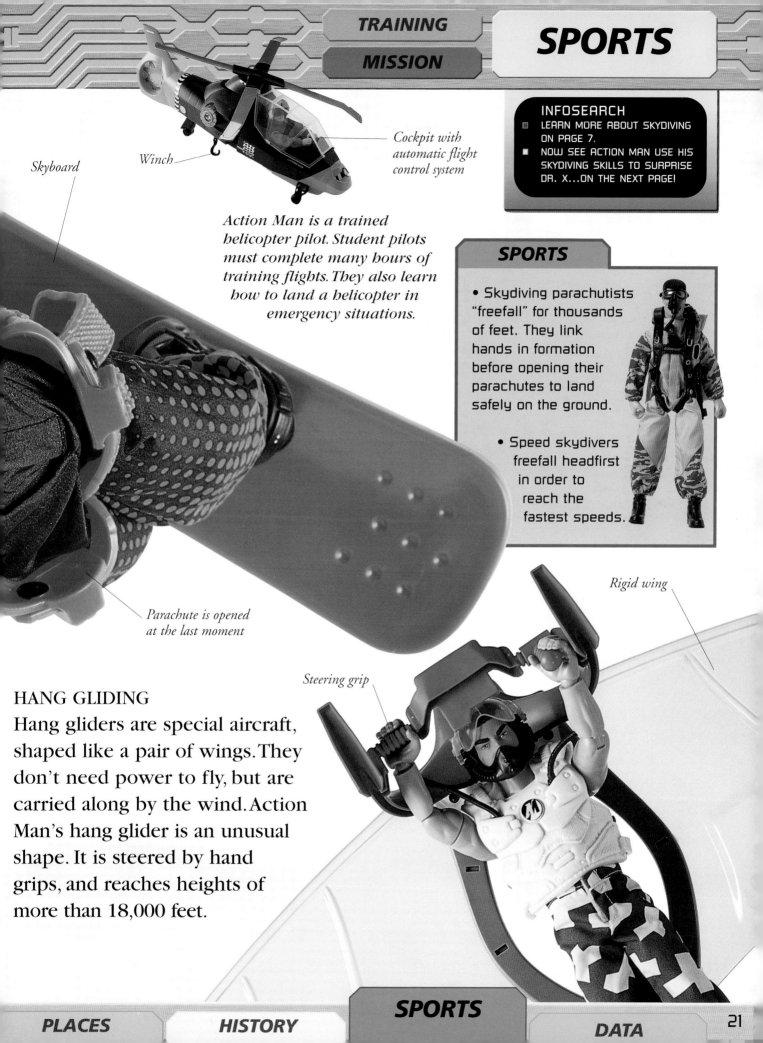

Action Man leapt from the plane. He straightened his body like an arrow. Seconds later he was falling at more than half the speed of sound! He pulled the rip cord on his parachute and made a perfect landing on the edge of a vast crater.

WOOOOSSHHH!

*Dr. X's volcanic island base*

*Action Man in speed skydiving position*

## Extreme mission

Action Man had rushed from his training as soon as he heard the news. Dr. X had threatened to set off all the world's volcanoes using his supercomputer. The result would be total meltdown! Only Action Man had the skills to skydive right onto Dr. X's volcanic island base.

## Into the volcano

Action Man spied the entrance to the base. He broke in and found an access point to the mainframe computer. He connected to it and found the codes that would set off the volcanoes. Just then, he heard the foul voice of Professor Gangrene...

"Action Man, how kind of you to die."

## Showdown

Gangrene escorted Action Man to Dr. X. "Action Man, you are just in time for the show. Watch me blow up the world!" He punched in a code on the computer. Just then, an explosion rocked the base. "Dr. X," said Action Man. "I reprogrammed your computer. The only volcano that's going to blow is this one."

"Watch the show."

MISSION DR X IN EXPLOSIVE MOOD
LOCATION PACIFIC OCEAN

### SPECIAL DATA

Main control room

SECRET PLAN OF DR. X'S BASE

VOLCANOES: MOST OF THE WORLD'S VOLCANOES LIE IN A BELT CALLED THE "RING OF FIRE," WHICH SURROUNDS THE PACIFIC OCEAN.

### MISSION STATS

SKYDIVING EQUIPMENT: BREATHING MASK AND PARACHUTE

FIDGIT: CAMERA OPERATOR

PROCEED

## Hotfooting it!

Just then, a wall blew out and red-hot volcanic lava spewed in. Action Man seized his moment. He raced down corridors, always one step ahead of the burning liquid that was bubbling all around. When he reached the open air, a helicopter was waiting. A line dropped and he was hoisted to safety, just as the base became a giant fireball. "Alright!" yelled Fidgit, as she aimed her camera. "Great work!"

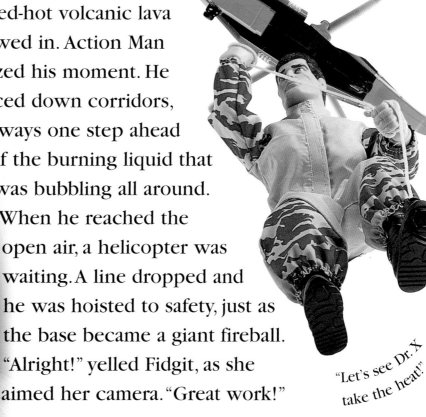

"Let's see Dr. X take the heat!"

Cities don't get much more extreme than Tokyo in Japan. It's fast-paced, high-tech, and super-modern. Many futuristic inventions come from Japan, including some amazing ways to race on two or four wheels. Let Action Man demonstrate them for you!

*Full-face crash helmet*

*Shock-absorbant framework*

*Tough wheels*

*Action Man's Superbike is ideal for narrow streets.*

## MINI-SPEEDER

This mini-speeder whizzes around a go-kart track as fast as a speeding car. A dozen or more speeders race at one time—drivers bump against each other to take the lead.

### PLACES

• Tokyo is the capital city of Japan. It is the world's largest city. Over 27 million people live and work there.

• In 2001, Tokyo hosted a junior version of the X Games for young extreme sports fanatics aged 10 to 14.

*This single-driver extreme sidecar is built for speed. Action Man lies forward on it to reduce wind resistance.*

INFOSEARCH
☐ CAN YOU GUESS WHICH CAR IS FASTER THAN THE SILVER SPEEDER? SEE PAGES 18-19.
■ FIND OUT ABOUT MARTIAL ARTS ON PAGES 26-27.

## WHEELS

Action Man takes inline skating to the next level with these motorized skates. He accelerates and brakes using the handheld cable control. The thick wheels allow him to skate on roads or across country. Watch this futuristic sport take off!

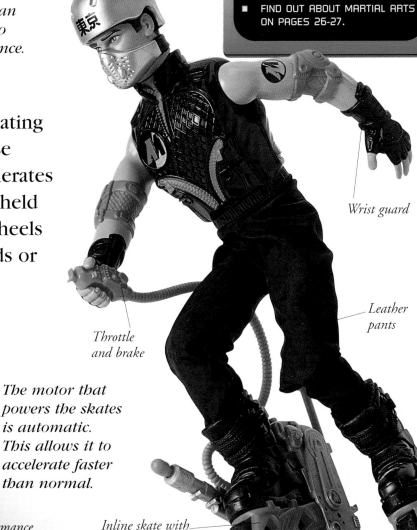

*Wrist guard*

*Leather pants*

*Throttle and brake*

*The motor that powers the skates is automatic. This allows it to accelerate faster than normal.*

*High-performance racing wheels*

*Inline skate with 200cc engine*

### EQUIPMENT

• Action Man cruises Tokyo in his Silver Speeder. This super-sleek vehicle is powerful and fast, and can accelerate to top speed in a matter of seconds.

• The Silver Speeder has a secret missile system hidden under the hood. Action Man can launch a couple of shots to slow down Dr. X in a car chase.

*Open top*

*Mirror windshield*

*Racing tires*

Martial arts experts are as fast as lightning! They jump, kick, and spin with expert timing. Martial arts began hundreds of years ago in the countries of East Asia. They are used for self-defense and sport. It takes a lot of training to be a master like Action Man.

*Eyes focused on target*

*Loose jacket called a "gi"*

*Short pants*

*Heel aimed toward target*

*Headband*

HIGH-ENERGY JUMP
Flying high jumps are an important part of many martial arts, including karate and tae kwon do. In tae kwon do contests, athletes win points for skillful moves against their opponent.

*Action Man trains with martial arts experts. He learns ninja spy skills such as how to move silently and stay totally still for a long time.*

*Protective top*

*Short staff for sparring*

## HISTORY

- In ancient Japan, the mysterious and feared ninjas were master spies. Their skills were believed to be almost magical.

- They made daring raids into enemy lands to find out information or to sabotage defenses. Then they escaped as silently as they had come.

- Ninjas used special hand signals to communicate to one other in secret.

*Ninja stealth move*

NINJA HAND SIGNAL

**HISTORY**     **SPORTS**     **EQUIPMENT**     **NATURE**

**INFOSEARCH**
- ☐ WHERE DOES KUNG FU COME FROM? FIND OUT ON PAGE 7.
- ☐ CHECK OUT ABOUT ACTION MAN'S HIGH-TECH TOKYO VEHICLES ON PAGES 24-25.

## TAE KWON DO

Tae kwon do is a modern martial art from Korea. It is similar to Japanese karate, with amazing flying jumps.

## JUDO

In the Japanese martial art Judo, grappling techniques are used to trip or throw an opponent. Points are awarded for good throws.

## AIKIDO

Aikido is a grappling art from Japan. Players use a range of special moves to overcome an opponent.

## SHAOLIN

The Shaolin monks are famous for their fighting abilities. Lots of martial arts grew from their skills.

## THAI BOXING

Thai boxing is the national sport of Thailand. It is similar to Western boxing except that kicks, throws, and knee and elbow strikes are allowed.

## KARATE

Karate is a fighting sport that relies mostly on skilled high-energy strikes. It began on the Japanese island of Okinawa.

RUSSIA

MONGOLIA

NORTH KOREA

SOUTH KOREA

CHINA

JAPAN

INDIA

BURMA

OKINAWA

TAIWAN

LAOS

THAILAND

PHILIPPINES

CAMBODIA

VIETNAM

PACIFIC

OCEAN

MALAYSIA

*Protective headgear*

*Action Man demonstrates a kick boxing stance. This sport is influenced by Thai boxing.*

*Strap-on boots protect feet*

Jungles are hot, sticky, and crawling with insects. Yet many people live here. Food and water are all around... if you know where to look.

Action Man likes to train in the jungle. Like all extreme sports fanatics, he is always on the lookout for the perfect cliff to climb or river to kayak down.

*Body paint helps Action Man hide in the jungle*

*Bamboo blowpipe*

## HUNTING TOOL

Blowpipes are accurate and powerful hunting devices. They are used by some jungle tribes. Action Man learned many useful jungle skills when he spent some time living with a remote tribe in South America.

*Dart for blowpipe*

*Action Man uses this disguised trap to guard his secret base. It looks just like a jungle plant. But if Dr. X is on the prowl—watch out!*

*Trap shuts when it is stepped on*

### PLACES

• Jungles are also known as tropical rain forests. This is because it rains here nearly every day! More types of animals and plants live in tropical rain forests than anywhere else on Earth.

• Rain forests are under threat from people cutting them down for wood. In Central America, 90 percent of the rain forest has gone.

- Many jungle animals and plants are very dangerous. The skin of the poison dart frog is highly toxic.

- Some jungle hunters put the poison on the tips of their blowpipe darts.

**NATURE**

*Action Man keeps a lookout*

*Rope to tow jeep out of mud*

*Equipment storage*

INFOSEARCH
☐ WHERE ARE JUNGLES FOUND? SEE PAGES 6-7.
■ SEE ACTION MAN USING A BOW AND ARROW ON PAGE 30.
■ CAN YOU GUESS WHO IS ALSO LURKING IN THE JUNGLE? TURN THE PAGE TO FIND OUT...

*Rear-mounted engine*

*Heavy tread tires*

*Reinforced front end pushes obstacles aside*

*Headband keeps sweat out of eyes*

## JUNGLE JEEP

Action Man drives a powerful off-road jeep. It can handle almost any driving conditions, including mud and water. It even has a special rope on the front to pull out the vehicle if it gets stuck in mud. Action Man uses his jungle jeep to carry his sports equipment, tent, and supplies.

*Climbing vine*

**HEALTH**

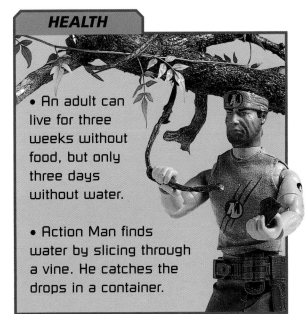

- An adult can live for three weeks without food, but only three days without water.

- Action Man finds water by slicing through a vine. He catches the drops in a container.

## CLIMBING

To escape danger or to see where you are, you might need to climb a tree. Action Man uses a length of vine and special spiked boots to help him climb more easily.

# JUNGLE FACE-OFF

**A**ction Man was working on his archery skills in the Central American rain forest. One morning he received reports of activity deep in the forest. Could it be Dr. X? He decided to investigate. The only way to travel that far into the jungle was by river, so he climbed aboard his log raft.

## Curious footprints

Action Man reached a mysterious part of the jungle. Crumbling temples and giant stone heads lay all around. He noticed some footprints. They led toward a stone head with one red eye. As Action Man approached, the ground suddenly fell away and sharp sticks shot up. "A trap!" he said. "Someone doesn't want visitors."

*TWAAAANG!*

*High-tension bow*

*Jungle plants*

## One in the eye

"There must be a way in," thought Action Man, "because the footprints lead up to the statue." Then he had an idea. He aimed his bow at the red eye...

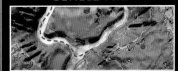

MISSION THE RETURN OF DR. X
LOCATION CENTRAL AMERICA

### JUNGLE MAP

MORE THAN 1,000 YEARS AGO, THE MAYAN PEOPLE BUILT MANY TEMPLES AND STATUES IN CENTRAL AMERICA. THEY CAN STILL BE SEEN TODAY.

PROCEED

*Stone door slides open*

## Old foes meet

As the arrow hit, a grinding sound filled the air, and the statue's face slid open. Dr. X and Gangrene stood inside, shaking with anger. "So you thought you'd seen the last of me when you destroyed my volcano base," snorted Dr. X. "But, as you can see, I have returned!" Then, in a moment, they were gone...

*Lucky arrow*

*Sharpened sticks in pit trap*

H ow high can you go? For extreme climbers, the answer is: all the way to the top. Climbers are fanatical about tackling the most difficult rock faces. The challenge is all about achieving the nearly impossible.

*Equipment harness*

*"ALTITUDE WITH ATTITUDE!"*

## ROCK CLIMBING

Action Man grips onto a rock overhang with his bare hands. Rock climbers use specialized gear. As they go up, they hammer special pins called anchors into the rock. Then they fasten ropes through the anchors. These ropes support the climbers if they fall.

*Climbing shoe*

*Action Man leaps over boulders at the top*

*Climbing shorts*

*Bouldering is the latest trend in sports climbing. The competitors move up rocks close to the ground. In this way the spectators can see all the action.*

### SKILLS

• Climbers must be in top shape, with a focused mind and good physical coordination.

• Climbing shoes are specially designed with soft rubber soles. They grip well to the rock.

**SKILLS**

**INFOSEARCH**
- WHERE ARE THE WORLD'S MOST MOUNTAINOUS AREAS? SEE PAGES 6-7.
- SEE ACTION MAN'S 4X4 MOUNTAIN JEEP ON PAGE 1.

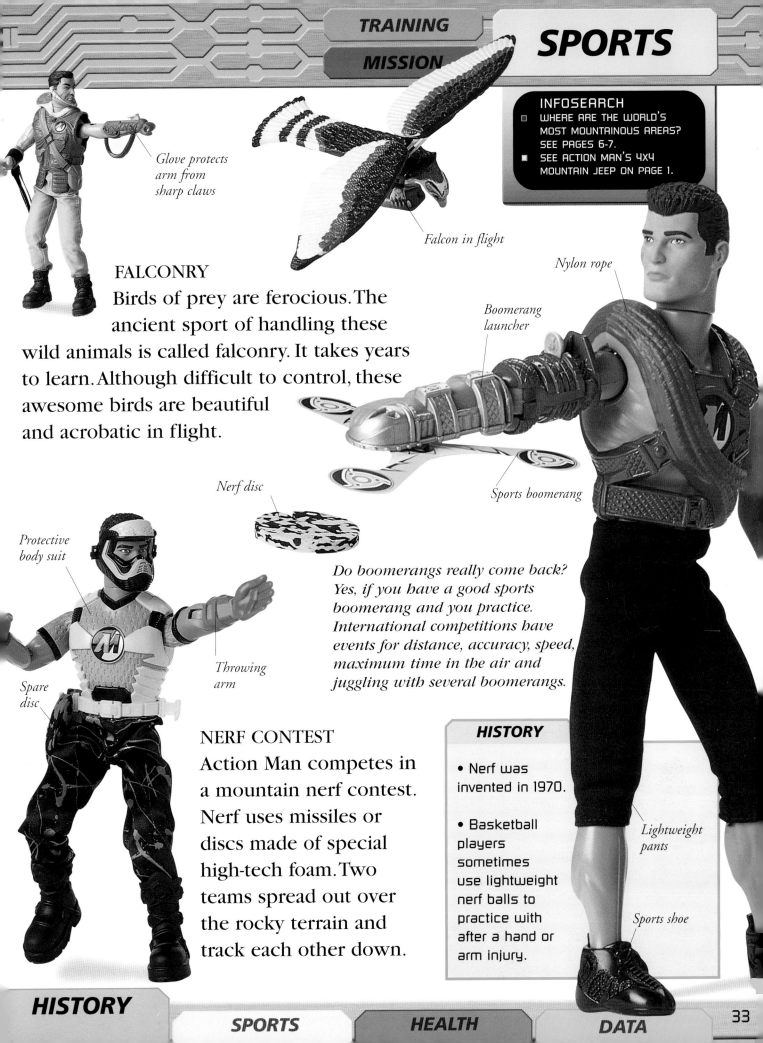

*Glove protects arm from sharp claws*

*Falcon in flight*

*Nylon rope*

*Boomerang launcher*

## FALCONRY
Birds of prey are ferocious. The ancient sport of handling these wild animals is called falconry. It takes years to learn. Although difficult to control, these awesome birds are beautiful and acrobatic in flight.

*Sports boomerang*

*Nerf disc*

*Protective body suit*

*Do boomerangs really come back? Yes, if you have a good sports boomerang and you practice. International competitions have events for distance, accuracy, speed, maximum time in the air and juggling with several boomerangs.*

*Throwing arm*

*Spare disc*

## NERF CONTEST
Action Man competes in a mountain nerf contest. Nerf uses missiles or discs made of special high-tech foam. Two teams spread out over the rocky terrain and track each other down.

### HISTORY

- Nerf was invented in 1970.

- Basketball players sometimes use lightweight nerf balls to practice with after a hand or arm injury.

*Lightweight pants*

*Sports shoe*

# DESERT TRAINING

*Scarf protects face and neck from sun*

In the desert, only the strong survive. This is why Action Man trains there. Deserts are blazing hot by day and freezing cold at night. There is very little food and water. You have to learn how to be better than nature.

## PLACES

• *Thrust SSC* is the fastest car in the world. In 1997, it shot across the Black Rock Desert, Nevada, at a speed of 763 mph.

*Cactus used for target practice*

*Goggles protect eyes from sun*

*Twin-ball launcher requires great skill to handle*

## TWIN-BALL LAUNCHER

Action man is testing out a new machine. It is a high-powered twin-ball launcher. It fires two balls joined by rope, which wrap tightly around targets. One day, Action Man might need to use this to stop Dr. X.

*Desert boots help keep feet cool*

*Two-way radio*

## HEALTH

• In an emergency, Action Man finds water in a cactus. He cuts off the top and sucks out the juice using a hollow reed.

• Action Man keeps cool under a makeshift tent. It is made by tying a length of string between two rocks and hanging a blanket over it.

*Blanket*

*Standing rock*

Action Man goes running in the desert only in the early morning and evening. At other times, the sun is too hot. He radios in to base camp regularly for extra safety.

*Rope winch can be used to tow jeep out of soft ground*

## CROSSING THE DESERT

A serious desert expedition calls for a powerful jeep to carry all the heavy equipment and supplies. Deserts are hazardous to cross. Sandy ground can vary from a firm, flat surface to deep, soft dunes. It is best to drive slowly, looking out for boulders up ahead that could damage the underside of the engine.

INFOSEARCH
- WHERE IN THE WORLD ARE DESERTS FOUND? TO FIND OUT, SEE PAGES 6-7.
- TURN THE PAGE TO SEE THE TRAP DR. X HAS SET FOR ACTION MAN...

*Sun hat with neck protection*

*Bulky equipment carried on roofrack*

*Two-seat vehicle*

*Four-wheel drive engine gives jeep extra power to get out of soft ground when stuck*

*Desert boots with thick soles*

*Chunky tires for rough ground*

HEALTH

# TOMB OF THE PHARAOHS

Action Man had tracked Dr. X to Egypt, the land of the ancient pharaohs. His secret hideout was a ruined tomb that stood beside the Nile River. Action Man wanted to surprise Dr. X by making a silent approach by water using a crocodile disguise. Meanwhile... somewhere in the skies above Action Man, a stealth helicopter flew by. Inside, a deranged figure with a shaved head and a mechanical arm was laughing. "Ha, ha, ha! Perfect! Action Man is walking right into my trap."

*"This is some snappy disguise!"*

*Decorated coffins*

**CREEEEEK!**

CREEPY COFFINS
Back on the ground, Action Man approached the tomb. He carried a net-trapper in order to catch Dr. X once and for all. Inside the temple, he entered an entrance hallway lined with painted coffins. As he crept past, Action Man had the uncanny impression that he was being watched...

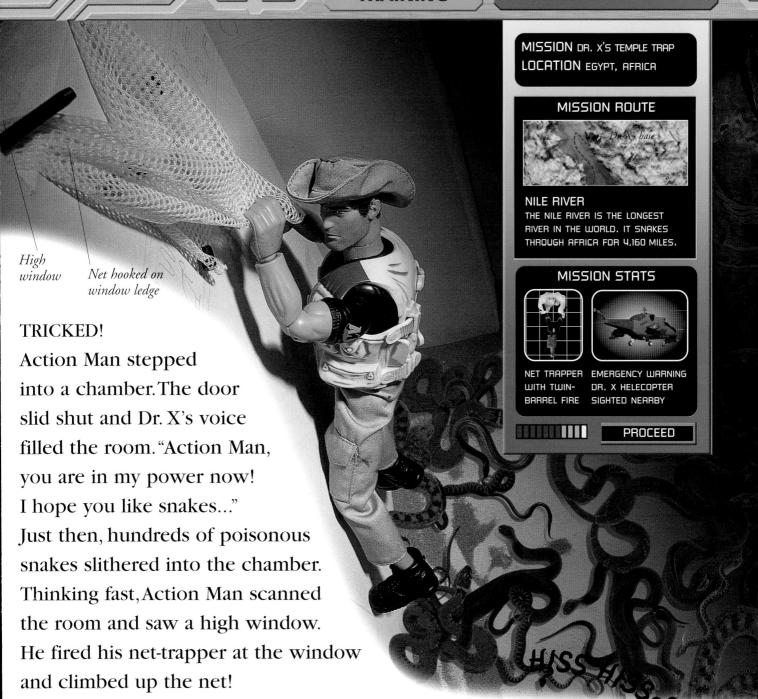

MISSION DR. X'S TEMPLE TRAP
LOCATION EGYPT, AFRICA

### MISSION ROUTE

*Dr. X's base*

**NILE RIVER**
THE NILE RIVER IS THE LONGEST
RIVER IN THE WORLD. IT SNAKES
THROUGH AFRICA FOR 4,160 MILES.

### MISSION STATS

NET TRAPPER    EMERGENCY WARNING
WITH TWIN-     DR. X HELECOPTER
BARREL FIRE    SIGHTED NEARBY

PROCEED

*High
window*

*Net hooked on
window ledge*

## TRICKED!

Action Man stepped
into a chamber. The door
slid shut and Dr. X's voice
filled the room. "Action Man,
you are in my power now!
I hope you like snakes..."
Just then, hundreds of poisonous
snakes slithered into the chamber.
Thinking fast, Action Man scanned
the room and saw a high window.
He fired his net-trapper at the window
and climbed up the net!

HISS-HISS-SSS

### THE MUMMY STRIKES

Action Man found his way back to the entrance
hallway. Suddenly, one of the coffins opened and a
mummy lunged out. It was Maxx, Dr. X's bandage-
faced ally. Action Man pushed lots of coffins into
Maxx's path to hold him back. "Dr. X wins this
round," said Action Man, as he escaped the tomb.

# EXTREME WATER SPORTS

*Face mask*

It's time to sink or swim! Extreme water sports are the wildest, weirdest way to get wet. Contestants race over the sea in super-fast mini-hovercraft or battle their way down steep mountain rivers in kayaks.

*Fast, jet-powered hydrospeeders fly across the water.*

*Air tank*

*Buoyancy converter helps diver float on water surface*

## SCUBA DIVING

Divers use scuba gear to swim underwater for periods of time. This equipment allows them to breathe air from a tank. Record-breaking dives of 295 feet have been recorded—about the length of a football field.

*Propeller*

*Action Man races in a one-person hovercraft. These craft can travel over land and sea. They float on a cushion of air. Many countries hold hovercraft-racing championships.*

**NATURE**

- The underwater world is one of the most extreme locations on Earth.

- Scuba divers set themselves challenges such as exploring underwater caves or ancient shipwrecks.

INFOSEARCH
- LEARN ABOUT AN EXTREME KAYAKING LOCATION ON PAGE 6.
- TO FOLLOW ACTION MAN AS HE DISCOVERS DR. X'S UNDERWATER BASE, TURN THE PAGE...

EXTREME KAYAKING
White-water rafters paddle down fast-moving mountain rivers in kayaks (or canoes). Rivers are rated according to how difficult they are to navigate. The most extreme rating is VII (seven). The water in these rivers crashes its way around giant rocks and over very steep drops. In this sport, a hard helmet is a definite must-have!

*The canoeist sits inside with legs outstretched*

*Kayaks are designed to be lightweight but tough*

*Rapids (fast-flowing river water over rocks)*

## SPORTS

• Kayaks were first used by Inuits, an ancient people who live in parts of Alaska, Canada, and Greenland.

• Kayaks can handle just about any fast-moving water when paddled skillfully.

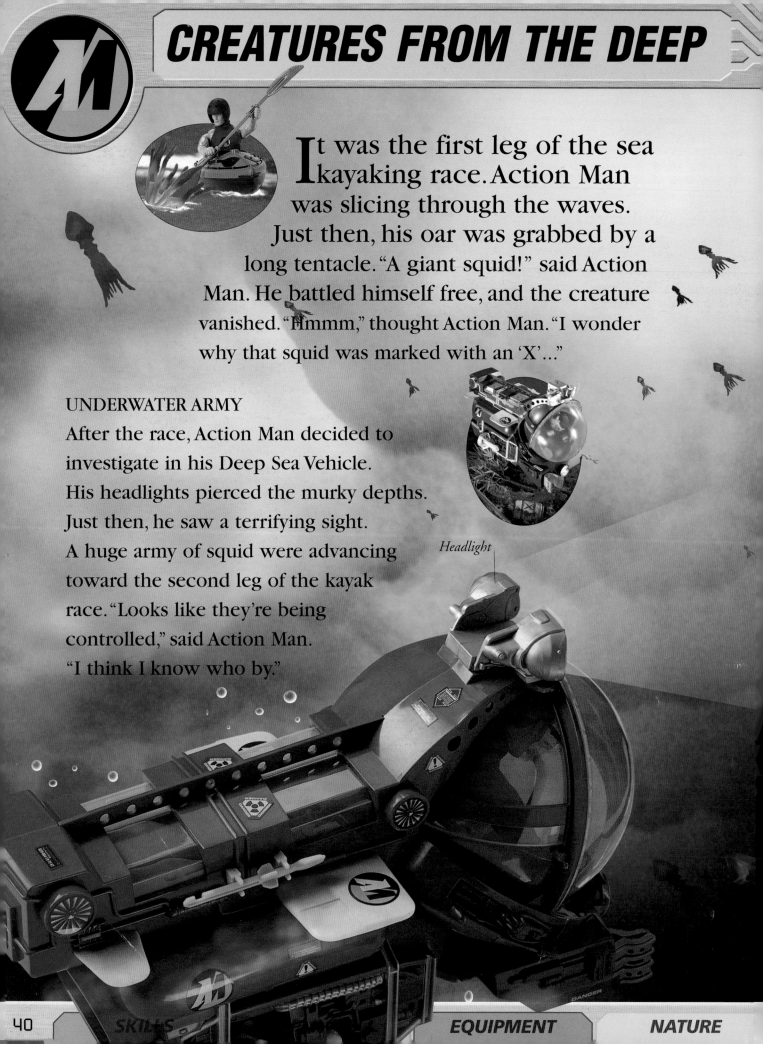

It was the first leg of the sea kayaking race. Action Man was slicing through the waves. Just then, his oar was grabbed by a long tentacle. "A giant squid!" said Action Man. He battled himself free, and the creature vanished. "Hmmm," thought Action Man. "I wonder why that squid was marked with an 'X'..."

## UNDERWATER ARMY

After the race, Action Man decided to investigate in his Deep Sea Vehicle. His headlights pierced the murky depths. Just then, he saw a terrifying sight. A huge army of squid were advancing toward the second leg of the kayak race. "Looks like they're being controlled," said Action Man. "I think I know who by."

Headlight

## IN DEEP WATER

Suddenly Action Man saw a sinister object emerging from the darkness. "Dr. X's submarine!" he gasped. "I knew Dr. X would be in charge of this fiendish army. I must stop him." Cautiously, Action Man slipped alongside the enemy sub.

*Dr. X's submarine*

**MISSION** DR. X'S SQUID ARMY
**LOCATION** INDIAN OCEAN

### ACTION MAN'S ROUTE

*Location of Dr. X's sub*

**SEABED**
THE SEABED MOSTLY LIES 4 MILES BELOW THE SURFACE. SOME OCEAN TRENCHES ARE 6.8 MILES DEEP.

### MISSION STATS

DEEP SEA VEHICLE FEATURES: HIGH-OUTPUT ENGINE, GRABBING CLAW

DR. X SUB FOUND IN DEEP SEA

PROCEED

## SABOTAGE

Action Man located the sub's oxygen supply. Inside, a warning siren blared out. Dr. X peered out of a porthole and saw Action Man holding the severed air pipe in his vehicle's grabbing claw. "That should force him up for air," said Action Man.

*"I'll get you next time..."*

SNAAAAP!

Extreme sports fanatics live for winter. Some of the fastest, most exciting sports take place on snow and ice. Extreme snowboarders and skiers invent new challenges and fresh tricks all the time. But whatever the sport, Action Man stands out.

*Sunglasses reduce glare of the sun*

*Backpack with spare clothing, food, and tool kit*

*Waterproof jacket*

*"JUMP ON BOARD!"*

## SNOWBOARDING

Action Man lives out every snowboarder's dream – racing over fresh, untouched snow. Racing is just one style of snowboarding. Another type is called freestyle. This is all about gravity-defying aerial tricks and spins. Many snowboarding tricks were first perfected on skateboards.

*Ice pick for climbing up frozen cliffs*

*Snowboard*

### EQUIPMENT

• Snowboarding began in the US as long ago as the 1960s.

• Boards are made mostly of tough-but-light fiberglass.

• Snowboarders wear boots that clip securely onto the snowboard.

*Boot fastening*

*Action Man's board sports a unique design*

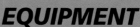

*Action Man climbs up steep ice walls using his blades...*

*... and when danger strikes he's prepared!*

## SPEED SKATING

When Action Man skates on ice, he goes so fast, his body is a blur. Extreme ice sports competitions are a thrilling challenge. Over the course of several miles, competitors must skate at high speed and then climb solid walls of ice.

### INFOSEARCH
- WHERE IN THE WORLD DO SNOWBOARDING COMPETITIONS TAKE PLACE? SEE PAGES 6-7.
- JUST HOW EXTREME IS THE SPORT OF ICE RACING? SEE PAGE 17.

*Wrist guard*

*Chrome-plated ice blade*

*Quick-release strap*

## FREERIDE SKIING

Regular skiers twist and turn down snowy slopes. Extreme skiers do their twisting and turning high in the air! They launch themselves off ramps to do "big airs" (airborne stunts).

*Thermal mask*

*Competition number*

*Titanium ski pole*

*Waterproof lightweight fabric*

*High-tech skis*

*High-visibility clothing*

*Ski boots*

### SPORTS

- Freestyle is the wild side of skiing. The sport has only recently been allowed into the Olympic Games.

- This extreme sport tests a skier's nerve to the maximum. Skiers compete to perform the most awesome stunts.

Those who compete in winter sports need be in good shape. Snow is very tiring to walk on, and there are many dangers. These risks include snow storms, deep crevasses, and frostbite (when the body is damaged by the cold). To survive, you need the right clothing and equipment.

*Wings fold up onto shoulder harness*

*Paraglider wing*

*Thermal jumpsuit*

*Skis*

Action Man soars through the air on his paraglider. When he lands, he folds up the wings and uses his skis.

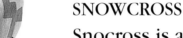

*Action Man on training mission*

## SNOWCROSS
Snocross is a sport in which competitors race snow mobiles. They zip over the snow at high speed, and use ramps to take off into the air. Snow mobiles move on caterpillar tracks and are steered like a motorcycle.

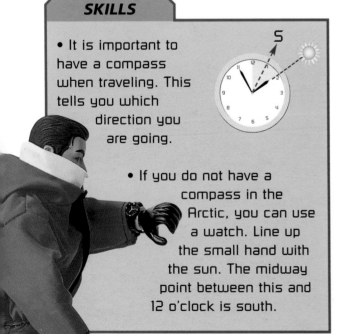

### SKILLS

• It is important to have a compass when traveling. This tells you which direction you are going.

• If you do not have a compass in the Arctic, you can use a watch. Line up the small hand with the sun. The midway point between this and 12 o'clock is south.

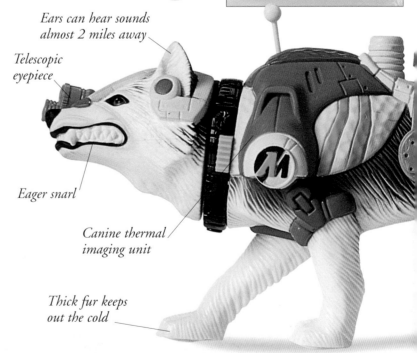

*Ears can hear sounds almost 2 miles away*

*Telescopic eyepiece*

*Eager snarl*

*Canine thermal imaging unit*

*Thick fur keeps out the cold*

## SURVIVAL

• Action Man takes shelter in an igloo, built from blocks of hard snow. The heat from his body warms up the air inside the igloo. Soon it is very warm.

INFOSEARCH
☐ SEE ACTION MAN TRAINING IN THE DESERT ON PAGES 34-35.
☐ WHAT IS DR X DOING AT THE NORTH POLE? TURN THE PAGE TO FIND OUT...

*Smooth ice surface*

*Entrance tunnel*

• The Arctic is a gigantic frozen ocean surrounding the North Pole. It is the most remote, hostile place on Earth.

*Hood can be used to cover the face in a blizzard*

*Insulated jacket*

## ARCTIC EXPLORER

Action Man's sled is pulled by a trained wolf (code name: Blizzard). Blizzard moves quickly across the snow and is incredibly tough. He is also good company on long journeys.

*Steering bars*

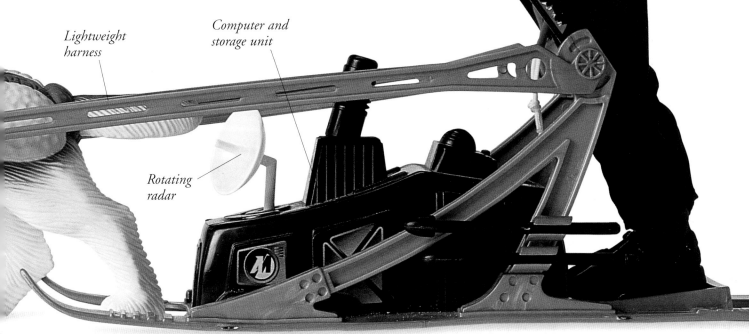

*Lightweight harness*

*Computer and storage unit*

*Rotating radar*

## SURVIVAL

Action Man hit the throttle on his snow scooter and picked up speed. He was racing in the snowy wilderness of the North Pole, where the Acceleration Games were being held. Suddenly, the scooters in front skidded violently off the course. It was as if they had been pulled by a strong force. Then Action Man himself was thrown into the snow.

HUMMMMMM!

Ice walls

Blizzard stays out of sight

Action Man is held in the air by the force of Dr. X's supermagnet

## Investigations

Later, Action Man set out to investigate the incident. He took his sled pulled by Blizzard the wolf. When he reached the spot, the sled's dials spun around. "It's a huge magnetic force," said Action Man.

## Into the ice cave

Action Man followed the source of the magnetic beam to an ice cave. He sneaked along the icy corridors. Then he heard a familiar voice muttering "... my supermagnet will soon change the location of the magnetic North Pole. Navigation will be thrown into chaos."

Lever controls
direction of
magnetic field

Control panel for
the supermagnet

The super-
magnet

MISSION MAGNETIC DISRUPTION
LOCATION THE NORTH POLE

### ACTION MAN'S ROUTE

Race circuit

Dr. X's base

MAGNETIC NORTH POLE
COMPASS NEEDLES ALWAYS POINT
TO MAGNETIC NORTH. THIS HELPS
TRAVELERS FIND THEIR WAY.

### MISSION STATS

POLAR MISSION SLED
FEATURES: SATELLITE
NAVIGATION EQUIPMENT

BLIZZARD
TRAINED
WOLF

PROCEED

Tank of
poisonous gas

CLUNK!

## Final showdown

Action Man burst in. Dr. X saw him and
quickly pulled a lever. Action Man was held in
the air by a strong force. He couldn't move. "Ha!" sneered
Dr. X. "My supermagnet has many uses." Luckily, Blizzard was
still hiding. He leapt at the magnet lever. Now Dr. X flew into
the air. His metal arm had been caught in the magnetic field!

LONDON, NEW YORK, DELHI, PARIS, MUNICH, AND JOHANNESBURG

AUTHOR / SENIOR EDITOR  Simon Beecroft

PROJECT DESIGNER / SET BUILDER  Guy Harvey

ART DIRECTOR  Cathy Tincknell

PUBLISHING MANAGER  Cynthia O'Neill

PHOTOGRAPHER  Trish Gant

US EDITORS  Gary Werner and Margaret Parrish

PICTURE RESEARCHERS  Jo Haddon and Rachel Hilford

DTP DESIGNER  Andrew O'Brien

PRODUCTION  Nicola Torode

First American Edition, 2001

01 02 03 04 05 10 9 8 7 6 5 4 3 2 1

First published in the United States by
DK Publishing, Inc.
95 Madison Avenue
New York, New York 10016

Library of Congress Cataloging-in-Publication Data

Beecroft, Simon.
   Action man extreme sports / written by Simon Beecroft ; photography
by Trish Gant.– 1st American ed.
   p. cm.
   ISBN 0-7894-7907-9
   1. Extreme sports–Juvenile literature. [1. Extreme sports.]    I.
Title: Extreme sports. II. Gant, Trish, ill. III. Title.
   GV749.7 .B44 2001
   796.04–dc21
                                          2001028509

Color reproduction by Colourscan, Singapore
Printed and bound by L.E.G.O SpA, Italy

## PICTURE CREDITS
t=top, b=bottom, l=left, r=right, c=center
Bruce Coleman Ltd: 42br (Bruce Coleman Inc), endpapers (Taffan Widstrand); Corbis: 6br, 7tc, 7cr, 7bl, 13br, 22tl,
27tl, 27cla, 27clb, 32bl, 39br, 43br; 45t (Galen Rowell); Empics Ltd: 17tc; Werner Forman Archive: 26bc (Ninja
Museum, Ueno); Image Bank: 41crb, 12c (A T Willett), 6tl (Alan Becker); Oxford Scientific Films: 40-41 (Norbert Wu);
Powerstock Photolibrary / Zefa: 20bl; Sporting Pictures (UK) Ltd: 7tl, 7bc, 13tr, 17bl, 27c, 27bl, 27bc, 6tr (Stefan
Hunziker); Thrust SCC: 34tr (Chris Rossi/Thrust SSC); University of Reading: Dept of Cybernetics: 11br; Woodfall
Wild Images: 22tl (Ted Mead).

DK Publishing, Inc. would like to thank:
Sharon Reeves at Hasbro Consumer Products; John Kelly for additional design work;
Andrew O'Brien for mission file maps; James Leng for model making advice

see our complete
catalog at
**www.dk.com**